Wha: Celtic Christianity?

by Elizabeth Culling

Priest-in-Charge, Cherry Burton, York

Senior Advisor in Rural Affairs, Diocese of York

GROVE BOOKS LIMITED
RIDLEY HALL RD CAMBRIDGE CB3 9HU

Contents

Some Books

N. Chadwick *The Age of the Saints in the Early Celtic Church* (Oxford, 1961), is an historical and sympathetic account of Celtic Christianity. Both this and the next work provide the essential historical account for understanding the context of Celtic Christianity.

L. Hardinge *The Celtic Church in Britain* (London, 1972). Another historical and scholarly work.

E. De Waal *A World Made Whole. Rediscovering the Celtic Tradition* (London, 1991). Provides historical background to a wealth of material designed to introduce readers to the Celtic tradition. It is a balanced approach to the subject, and sensitively written.

D. Adam *The Edge of Glory. Prayers in the Celtic Tradition* (London, 1985). Modern prayers which recapture the spirit of the Celtic tradition. Good for individual prayer and corporate worship. See also *The Cry of the Deer* (London, 1987), and *The Eye of the Eagle* (London, 1987). His latest book, *Power Lines*, incorporates insights from the Celtic tradition into modern prayers about the concerns of work.

C. Bamford and W. P. Marsh *Celtic Christianity. Ecology and Holiness* (Edinburgh, 1986) is an anthology of stories, songs and poems from the Celtic tradition, with a useful historical introduction, well worth exploring.

A. Carmichael *New Moon of the Seasons. Prayers from the Highlands and Islands* (Edinburgh, 1986). An anthology selected from Carmichael's own selection of the Celtic tradition, but reasonably representative nevertheless. A good introduction to the *Carmina Gaedelica*.

A. M. Allchin and E. De Waal, (eds.), *Threshold of Light. Prayers and Praises from the Celtic Tradition*, 'Enfolded in love series' ed. R. Llewelyn, (London, 1986). Extracts ancient and modern for daily meditation, arranged in pairs: a text from the Gaelic tradition alongside one from the Welsh. There are helpful notes on each at the end.

First Impression May 1993
Reprinted with corrections September 1994; July 1998
ISSN 0262-799X **ISBN** 1 85174 279 4

Introduction

To ask 'What is Celtic Christianity?' today is often not just a question about the history of Christianity. There is great interest in what is termed Celtic spirituality, but this interest is also causing concern. Celtic Christianity appeals today for all kinds of reasons: a search for roots; concern for the environment and the belief that the rural world of the Celts was more in touch with Creation; the feeling that the Celts practised an undogmatic, mystical religion emphasizing the experience of God's presence every where, and so on.

The terms 'Celtic' and 'spirituality' both require some definition at the outset because of the ambiguities surrounding them. Celtic here is understood as applying to the geographical regions of Ireland, Scotland, Wales, Cornwall, Brittany and the Isle of Man. By the end of the seventh century, however, the influence of the Celtic Church stretched from the Firth of Forth to the Thames estuary. The emphasis is on Ireland, since most of what can be said about Christianity here also applies to the other Celtic lands, and it is the most well documented area. The time boundaries are from the mission of St. Patrick in AD 432 to the coming of the Anglo-Normans to Ireland in 1169.

Spirituality is a word that does not necessarily have a Christian foundation. Celtic spirituality has thus been interpreted very broadly by different writers, some of whom go far beyond the bounds of Christian orthodoxy. Some of the confusion arises from the mists of obscurity which enshroud the historical evidence concerning the Celts. Their culture predates Christianity and pagan beliefs continued to exist following its arrival in Celtic lands. Portraits such as the following occur: 'In the so-called Dark Ages a religion flourished in the islands of Britain which had more in common with Buddhism than with the institutional Christianity of the West.' [1]

In what follows 'spirituality' will be given a specifically Christian interpretation, denoting the living out of one's belief about and experience of God, as known through Jesus Christ. I will argue that some of what passes for Celtic spirituality arises more from wishful thinking than from a historical picture of the Celtic Christians. But can the truth now be discovered? This study is offered first as a means of exploring more of the riches of our Christian inheritance in the belief that there is much here to recover and learn from. Secondly, it is intended as an aid to discernment amidst a confusing array of spiritualities claiming to be authentically Celtic and Christian. The aim is practical and in the final section there are suggestions as to how Celtic Christianity can enlarge and inform our vision of God and help us shape a spirituality for today.

---

1   S Toulson *The Celtic Alternative* (London, 1986) Introduction.

2
Interpreting Spirituality from the Past

The modern interest in spirituality includes much that is backward-looking; wistful attempts to recapture a golden age of spiritual wholeness and authentic experience. Certain periods of history are singled out as holding the key to understanding our own age and one of the most popular is the era of the Celtic Church. There is no doubt that a great deal of romantic illusion surrounds the Celts. Cards and jewellery based on Celtic art, music and songs in the Celtic style, prayers in the Celtic tradition and pilgrimages to places connected with the ancient Celtic world abound in Christian circles of all kinds. Celtic spirituality is portrayed as non-institutional, creation-centred and cosmic in scope, stressing the feminine and the mystical. It is presented as a lost ideal, a missed opportunity in the history of the Church in Britain, and awaiting recovery in our own day.

But what in fact is the Celtic tradition? What are its historical and theological boundaries? Did it ever really exist, and can we claim to be connecting up with a living tradition in direct descent from the early Celtic Church? Or is it part of the New Age conspiracy, an all-embracing enigma with no solid core, merely consisting of whatever one happens to fancy to be in tune with today's search for meaning?

J. P. Mackey, the editor of one book on Celtic Christianity, describes the criterion he uses to determine authentic Celtic Christianity as 'whatever seems to reverberate within some depths of my own Celtic consciousness'.[2]

If this kind of criterion is used to sift the evidence of history, subjectivity inevitably takes over. Thus, in spite of hard evidence to the contrary, a writer like Mackey is free to build up a picture of Celtic Christianity as characterized by a theology which excludes original sin and a natural world which is 'altogether good and salvific' for 'the Celtic mentality'.[3]

Whenever we approach the evidence of history in this manner there is a real danger that we will find what we are looking for. If we select only what 'reverberates' in our consciousness we inevitably recreate the past in our own image. There is a tendency to treat spirituality as enduring truth, outside historical circumstances. All spiritual traditions, however, have a context which has shaped and conditioned them. They are therefore all based on relative values and limited perspectives. To ignore this is to miss the reason why a certain tradition contains particular emphases, or is expressed in a particular way. We cannot cut off the realm of spiritual experience from the concreteness of the world and history. Spirituality is about the way people have responded to God at different times

---

2   J P Mackey *An introduction to Celtic Christianity* (Edinburgh, 1988) Introduction.
3   ibid, loc cit.

and in different places. That is why different traditions exist. It is what makes the Celtic tradition distinctive.

Any period from the past has to be taken seriously on its own terms, other wise contemporary concerns will lead us to subordinate history to present meaning and significance. The result of seizing on what immediately appeals in an historical tradition is that we try to force it into our contemporary world-view and therefore ignore aspects which sound alien or counter to our own situation. The world of the Celts has been subjected to 'presentism', which collapses the past into the present. Thus contemporary concerns have overridden the necessary historical perspective so that the Celtic tradition has to some extent been re-invented. We can see this in the way in which key elements, dictated by present-day issues, such as concern for creation, have been perceived in the historical data. These have then been uncritically and anachronistically translated into the present.

If we only see what we want to see we are well on the way to escaping into an idealized past. We admire the closeness to nature enjoyed by the Celts, for example. We wish we could recapture it for ourselves, but not many of us would willingly exchange our material comforts for a Celtic monastery, in order to have an 'authentic' Celtic experience of the world!

There is another important factor affecting the current search for spiritual satisfaction. Alongside the interest in the spiritual traditions of the Church, there is a theological gap. Many who are turning to the older Christian traditions are either unfamiliar with, or reluctant to accept, the religious framework to which they belong. Interest in spiritual things is clearly more widespread to the numbers of people committing themselves to the Christian Church, and it may be that there is a feeling that, by looking to the past, one may have the experience without the demands. Lack of concern for a theological framework has doubtless contributed to the hijacking of Celtic spirituality by New Age enthusiasts. Most of the latter would probably be surprised to discover that the theology of the Celts was profoundly biblical. Belief and practice were inseparable to the Celtic mind, and they drew constantly on the scriptures to interpret their faith and apply it to life. Lifted out of context and stripped of its presuppositions, any tradition can be remoulded to mean whatever we desire, but it will bear little resemblance to the original.

As already noted, the word 'Celtic' covers a whole culture which includes pagan and pre-Christian elements, as well as the Celtic Church. Furthermore, the Celtic Christians did not reject Celtic culture in many instances, but chose to Christianize it. This can give rise to real confusion, since the ambiguities in the evidence lay it open to different interpretations. So when St. Columba said:

'My Druid is Christ, the son of God, Christ, the Son of Mary, the Great Abbot, The Father, the Son, and the Holy Ghost'[4]

---

4   Quoted in W P Marsh and C Bamford *Celtic Christianity, Ecology and Holiness* (Edinburgh, 1982) p 110

was he compromising with the druidic culture around him? Other stories which show him opposing the power of the druids in the name of Christ clarify his stance, but it is often claimed that the Celts adopted an uncritical, all-embracing approach to culture. This is contrasted with numerous other instances in the history of the Church where Christians have rejected the culture of their converts out of hand. There is clearly an important issue here, which touches on the blurred edges of contemporary interest in spiritual things. How far may we, for instance, meet New Agers where they are, and take them on towards the Gospel without compromising the name of Christ?

Trying to discern what the Celtic Church was really like, and what its adherents believed, is difficult because written records from the Celtic era itself are so few. Most documentary evidence comes from the seventh century onwards, by which time the Church was well rooted, and legends concerning its beginnings and the exploits of its heroes well-established. There are no classical texts to put us in touch with the spirit of the tradition, as there are with the English mystics or St. Ignatius. Most of the lives of the saints, and of the songs and poems were written much later, and what we have is therefore an interpretation of the period. The Celtic tradition we have inherited is in fact, more medieval and Victorian than original.

Much of what we know about the beginnings of Christianity in the British Isles comes from the pen of St. Bede, the great seventh century historian and biblical scholar from Jarrow in the North of England. He admired the Celtic saints enormously, but he wrote as a Roman Christian. He wrote after the Synod of Whitby in 663 when the Celtic tradition was forced to bow to that of Rome. Many Christians attracted by Celtic spirituality regard the episode as a disaster, perceiving the Church in Britain as going downhill thereafter, ossifying into an institution instead of retaining the free spirit and spontaneity of the Celts. Bede did not think this way. It is important, however, to remember when reading him, that he wrote from a particular perspective.

The writings of Bede are just one instance of historical material undergoing interpretation. This is the case for almost all the material concerning Celtic Christianity drawn upon today. Six volumes of songs and blessings were collected by Alexander Carmichael at the beginning of this century and are quoted everywhere in Celtic anthologies. They were collected orally, and the material had itself been passed on from one generation to another for hundreds of years. It is difficult not to think that it had undergone at least some adaptation during that time. Moreover, the selection of material was determined by Carmichael himself as he travelled around in search of whatever he could find.[5] What is at issue here is the question of the spirit of a tradition, and how far it is legitimate, and indeed possible, to recreate it in a later age.

---

5   A Carmichael Carmina Gadelica. Hymns and incantations with illustrative notes of words, rites and customs dying and obsolete (6 vols,Edinburgh from 1900). Only the first two volumes were published before Carmichael's death in 1912. The remaining four came later, edited by his daughter and grandson.

In spite of all the difficulties, I want to suggest that it is possible to look back and benefit from the history of the Church's spiritual tradition in general, and Celtic spirituality in particular. We can re-enter the spirituality of another age in a way that seeks to be faithful to history and relevant to the contemporary world. While the pitfalls outlined above warn us against placing any spiritual tradition in a realm above or beyond history, it does not follow that such a tradition cannot, like a good wine, in some sense travel across the centuries.[6]

It is important that we do make the effort to recover Christianity's past for one very good reason. Jesus was an historical figure, and Christianity is an historical faith. Christians are concerned to establish the historical truth about Jesus, and we should have the same concern for the story of his people. It matters what kind of picture of the Christian faith is being transmitted today, for it will have a bearing upon the Church's self-perception, and that in turn will be passed on to the Church of tomorrow. We shall now move to trace the history of the Celtic Church, and out of this to examine the key elements of Celtic spirituality as far as they can be discerned from the evidence available.

3
The Beginnings and Spread of Celtic Christianity

Beginnings

There were Christians in Ireland before the mission of St. Patrick in 432, as indeed in Wales and northern Britain. St. Ninian, who converted the southern Picts, is traditionally believed to have founded the monastery *Candida Casa* at Whithorn in southern Galloway in 397.

The faith was most probably established in Ireland through contacts with Gaul, and legend has it that Patrick, like Ninian before him, received training for his mission there. There was no tight control from Rome at this time, or uniformity of practice in Europe as a whole. Patrick, however, constantly reiterated his orthodoxy in his writings, and there is every reason to accept that what he spread in Ireland was the orthodox Christian faith.

A satisfactory answer to the more difficult question of what kind of Church he found already in existence in Ireland would help us to see why the Celtic Church developed in its own way. It was orthodox in doctrine but diverged

---

6   This comparison is made by P Sheldrake in *Spirituality and History* (London, 1991) p 85. I have drawn a good deal of the preceding discussion from this excellent study of the issues involved in interpreting the history of spirituality.

from the rest of Europe in organization and ritual. St. Columbanus, born *circa* 543, described the Irish people as 'living on the edge of the world', and no doubt the distance from Rome was a significant factor in the emerging distinctiveness of the Church. Neither the Roman empire nor the Roman Church penetrated here where life was rural, hierarchical and family-based. It was an heroic, tribal society. Each tribe was ruled by its own king, and over him was the high-king who claimed the sovereignty of the whole of Ireland.

The Church took over this pattern. The basic unit of organization was not the diocese but the monastery, and this was modelled on the self-contained communities of the landowners. St. Martin of Tours, (316 - 397), one of the founders of western monasticism, had recognized the possibilities of the monastery as a tool in evangelism which could work well in rural communities. His influence upon the development of Christianity in Britain was strong, touching Ireland, Scotland and Wales through the missionary monks who took the gospel there.

The monastery would be founded by a member of one of the great families and the head, who might or might not be a bishop, was an abbot chosen from the same founding family. Each monastery was independent, unlike the monasteries of the rest of Europe which were bound together by the Rule of St. Benedict. Irish monasteries had their own rules, four of which survive from the period before 800. The main thrust of the rules is the challenge to follow Christ; details concerning life in the monastic community taking second place. The Celtic monasteries shared many features with the Eastern Monastic tradition, especially its extreme asceticism. So strong was the monastic element in Celtic Christianity that Christ was sometimes referred to as 'the Abbot of the Blessed in heaven'. The monasteries became centres of learning and culture, and it was from here that the mission of the Celtic Church proceeded.

In time, the Celtic Church developed features common to the rest of the Church in the West, but early differences played an important part in spreading the gospel in these lands. Irish dioceses were much smaller than those in the Roman Church. Each petty kingdom had its own bishop, who bowed to the abbot's authority in whose monastery he resided and whose function was liturgical rather than administrative. In the end it was the lack of central authority which helped ensure that the Celtic Church gave way to the Roman version of the faith, but the Celts had distinct advantages well suited to the society in which they were established.

The Spread of Celtic Christianity

The story of the spreading of Christianity through the Celtic lands is an inspiring one. Many legends surround the events, but through them there emerges a clear picture of heroism and commitment to Christ.

In 565 St. Columba left Ireland and landed on the island of Iona with his companions and founded a monastery. From here missionaries went out all over the north of Britain, preaching and founding monasteries. These came under the authority of the abbot of Iona. It was from here that St. Aidan came to

Northumbria in response to a request from King Oswald. Aidan was given the island of Lindisfarne as his episcopal see and with the king often acting as interpreter, he and his companions spread the gospel in this part of Britain. Other missionaries went further afield. At the end of the sixth century, St. Columbanus went from the monastery of St. Comgall, Bangor, in Ireland to preach and found monasteries in Europe, the most famous at Bobbio in Italy founded in 612.

In the meantime there was another mission to convert the islands of Britain, this time sent from Rome by Pope Gregory the Great. St. Augustine, later the first archbishop of Canterbury, came to convert the Anglo-Saxons to Christianity in 597. It was this tradition which eventually became dominant in Britain. When the two sides met at Whitby in 663 to seek a resolution, the ostensible differences involved the dating of Easter and the style of the tonsure. In fact there were far deeper issues at stake which concerned questions of authority and organization. The triumph of Roman Christianity did not of course mean the overnight disappearance of the Celtic version. For some time afterwards, certain English churchmen regarded Christians of the Celtic tradition as schismatics, even as heretics, questioning the validity of their orders and thereby of their sacraments. Iona finally celebrated Easter the Roman way in 716, but even then Celtic practices died hard and its traditions continued to survive. This was helped by a literary flowering in Ireland in the eighth century: the writing of the 'Lives' of saints, martyrologies, rules and penitentials. From these we can glean a picture of the earlier Celtic Church, but already we are looking at Celtic Christianity through someone else's eyes, and interpretation has begun.

4
The Basis of the Celtic Tradition

St. Patrick is the first figure of any substance that we can connect with the beginning of the Celtic Church of Ireland. We know about him from two texts: his own writings and later literature including two seventh century 'Lives', one by Tirechan, written *circa* 670 and the second by Muirchu written sometime before 700. Patrick's own writings consist of a letter to the soldiers of Coroticus reprimanding them for their treatment of his converts, and his *Confession*, a defence of his life and work.[7] It is a kind of spiritual autobiography and describes his conversion and later return to Ireland as a missionary. In it we can see the motivating force behind this tireless bishop who went around preaching, baptizing,

---

7   Translated and printed in N D O'Donoghue *Aristocracy of Soul. Patrick of Ireland* (London, 1987).

confirming, ordaining, educating, celebrating the eucharist, and attending to the economic and pastoral concerns of his flock.

As the *Confession* is the nearest thing we have to a classic text for the Celtic tradition, it seems an appropriate basis for a critique of Celtic spirituality. The rest of this chapter will concentrate on the content of the *Confession* in order to demonstrate the biblical and orthodox foundation of the early transmission of the Christian faith in Celtic Ireland.

Like the rest of Europe before the spread of Christianity, Irish society was thoroughly pagan, and this is made clear by the opposition to Patrick as he moved around the country preaching the Gospel. He mentions twelve dangers (unspecified) and numerous plots against him, and to read the later 'Lives' of this saint and of others, is to get a sense of spiritual as well as physical opposition to the work of evangelism. Patrick himself emerges as the implacable enemy of paganism on behalf of the Christ he serves:

'It was not my grace (1 Cor15.10), but God who conquered in me, . . . so that I came to the Irish peoples, to preach the Gospel, and to suffer insults from unbelievers; that I should listen to reproach . . . and endure many persecutions, even to chains.'[8]

Patrick was motivated by his understanding of the Christ he served, a vision formed from a combination of the scriptures and his own experience. To read the *Confession* is to detect a mind soaked in the scriptures. It was the source of Patrick's thinking and the foundation of his experience.

There is hardly a chapter where he does not quote directly or allude to scripture.

Patrick regards himself as the servant of Christ, and as honoured to be counted worthy to suffer for him. He frequently quotes or alludes to St. Paul in such a way as to suggest he modelled himself on the great apostle: he calls himself 'a sinner, the rudest and least of all the faithful' and is full of gratitude to God for his salvation.[9]

The most quoted book in the *Confession* is St. Paul's letter to the Romans. His sense of the grace of God is pervasive. Paul's confession in Timothy 1.13,14. 'I received mercy: I had acted ignorantly in unbelief, and the grace of our Lord overflowed for me with the faith and love that are in Christ Jesus' is echoed over and over by Patrick. Like Paul in parts of the New Testament, Patrick is defending himself against false charges and he adheres closely to the apologetic method and theological emphases of the apostle. It is significant that their common defence turns largely upon the doctrine of grace, for this confirms Patrick's understanding of the character of God and the place of redemption through Christ.

The initiative lies with God, and Patrick, like Paul, was called to be an ambassador for Christ in a hostile world, witnessing to the transforming power of the resurrection. Modelling himself on the great apostle in this way is of course

8 *Confession* p 37
9 op cit 1

a thoroughly evangelical practice, and a way of living out the Scriptures.

A deep, and at times mystical, sense of God's presence pervades Patrick's account. This is a feature which is often held to be one of the hallmarks of Celtic spirituality. Patrick records eight visions in his *Confession*. Their significance in the present context is that they focus on the person of Christ and arise out of Patrick's prayers and meditations on the scriptures:

' . . . after I had come to Ireland I daily used to feed cattle, and I prayed frequently during the day; the love of God and the fear of Him increased more and more, and faith became stronger, and the spirit was stirred; so that in one day I said about a hundred prayers, and in the night nearly the same; so that I used to remain in the woods and in the mountains; before daylight I used to rise to prayer, through snow, through frost, through rain and felt no harm; nor was there any slothfulness in me, as I now perceive, because the spirit was then fervent within me.'[10]

Here we see the ascetic streak and also the close association with the natural world which was later so prominent in Celtic spirituality. Equally important to notice in this context is the self-imposed discipline of Patrick as he grew in his faith. Through prayer, the scriptures, personal experience and service, his knowledge of Christ increased. His imitation of Christ is also worth noting. He sought out lonely places to pray, he modelled his work as bishop on the image of the Good Shepherd and in his sufferings he desired to be like Christ:

'I am prepared that He should give me "to drink of His cup" as He has granted to others that love Him. (Matt 20.22, 23)'.[11]

Like Christ he was tempted; like the Christ who emptied himself and became poor for our sake, he preferred poverty and calamity to riches and luxury.

He kept this vision before him, seeking to make Christ his own. As an ambassador for Christ, he was convinced he had received grace in order that others might receive salvation, and this placed him under a compulsion to live for Christ.

It remains to examine the dominant features of Patrick's portrayal of Christ. What emerges is a Christ who is both transcendent and immanent; transcendent in his role as judge and immanent in his sufferings.

Patrick refers to Christ as judge eight times in the *Confession*. Six of these are direct quotations from scripture, and one a paraphrase of Romans 14.10-12. The reality of heaven and hell and divine judgement were very apparent to Patrick, and Christ in his role as judge is an awesome figure. But the emphasis for Patrick is positive in the light of the Gospel he preached:

' . . . without doubt we shall rise in that day in the brightness of the sun that is in the glory of Jesus Christ, our Redeemer, as "sons of the living God" (Hosea 1.10), and "joint heirs with Christ" (Romans 8.17) and to be "conformable to His image" (Romans 8.29); for "Of Him, and through Him, and

10 *Confession* p 16
11 op cit p 57

in Him (Romans 11.36) we shall reign.'"[12]

The whole of the *Confession* sets out a high view of the person of Christ, but not one who is impersonal or remote. References to God's saving action in Christ are more numerous than to his judgment. Patrick knew in his own experience the mercy, the love and the protection of God. In all of this, God is near and not far off. It is in his consideration of his own sufferings and those of Christ, however, that the immanence of God is most telling.

Early on Patrick quotes from Philippians 2, and subsequently it is out of his own hardships that he understands the humanity of Christ. It is interesting that Patrick approaches the humanity of Christ from this angle rather than from the later images of 'Jesus the child of Mary' which subsequent Celtic prayers and poems stress.

5

How Orthodox was Celtic Christianity?

This is for many Christians the key question for today. I would suggest, however, that a subsequent question needs to be asked: how complete is the picture of Celtic Christianity offered by modern writers? For example, how many draw attention to the awesome transcendence of Christ the Judge to balance the immanence which is so often emphasized? The previous section set out the orthodoxy of St. Patrick, but he is one small part of a greater tradition, and we must take a wider view in order to answer the question of orthodoxy.

The Bible

The place of the Bible is one way of discerning the orthodoxy of any Christian tradition. St. Bede, himself described as 'that keen investigator of the Holy Scriptures', was quick to point out whether the people he was writing about were orthodox or not, and, although he was an avowed Roman, he admired the Celtic Christians for their zeal and orthodox doctrine.

In an article on St. Cuthbert, Sr. Benedicta Ward explains how two early biographers of the saint present a series of pictures of real events chosen for their significance in relation to God.[13] The writers use passages of Scripture which the saints knew and by which they lived, to illuminate the whole person. So, for example, when Cuthbert was about to die we see not a busy bishop seeking

---

12 *Confession* p 59
13 cf B Ward, 'The Spirituality of St Cuthbert' in Bonner et al (eds.) *St. Cuthbert, His Cult and His Community to AD 1200* (Durham,1989) pp 65-76.

nature's solitude 'away from it all', but a man crucified with Christ, alone, keeping silence as he accepts his approaching death.[14] The writers of the lives of the Celtic saints were interested in what linked them to the biblical tradition of holiness. Ward refers to the copy of the Lindisfarne Gospels placed over Cuthbert's tomb in Durham cathedral at the time of the eight hundredth anniversary of his death in 1987, as an image of the way his hagiographers placed the Scriptures over the life of their saint as they wrote.

The early Celtic Christians were thoroughly immersed in the scriptures. The survival of illuminated manuscripts and carved high crosses testifies to the love lavished on the Bible and to the honour in which it was held. In the monasteries, study played an important part in the monk's life. This consisted almost entirely of study of the scriptures. The Celts were avid copyists of the Bible and of commentaries, as later library catalogues show, such as that of the tenth century from the monastery of Bobbio. The monastery of Bangor, where Columbanus was professed as a monk, was noted for the scriptural basis of its life. A practical testimony to this love of scripture was the use of the pocket gospel book, a tradition which seems to have been unique to Ireland.

The consequence of such careful attention to the Bible was a spirituality which was balanced and orthodox both in content and expression. St. Patrick's *Confession*, as we have seen, is full of biblical references and allusions, testifying to the faith which Patrick passed on to his hearers, the first Celtic believers.

The Trinity

Following a strong affirmation of the Trinity, the hymn ascribed to St. Patrick, and known as 'St. Patrick's Breastplate' sets out a credal statement concerning Christ:

'I arise today
Through the strength of Christ's birth with His baptism,
Through the strength of His crucifixion with His burial,
Through the strength of His resurrection with His ascension,
Through the strength of His descent for the judgement of Doom.'[15]

As we have seen through the writings of St. Patrick, the figure of Christ was central to the Celts' understanding of God and the world. Christ was the motivator of the Celtic saints in all they did. At the same time, however, the Celts were deeply trinitarian in their understanding of God. They spoke of God the father and creator of the world; of God the Son, the loving friend and risen lord; and of God the Spirit who is at work in the world, pervading all of life with the divine presence and mediating between heaven and earth. Their trinitarianism comes across most clearly in the balanced rhythms of their poetry, which so often reflects on the persons of the Trinity in turn in order to draw attention to

14   cf B Colgrave (ed & trans) *Two Lives of St Cuthbert* (Camb 1940 repr 1985) IV, 11 pp 128-9.
15   There are two main versions of the 'Breastplate of St. Patrick' found in hymn books today. Both are quoted in full in D. Adam's book of meditations on its words *The Cry of the Deer* (London, 1987).

different aspects of God's character:

'I am bending my knee / In the eye of the Father who created me,
In the eye of the Son who died for me / In the eye of the Spirit who cleansed
me / In love and desire.'[16]

St. Patrick's Breastplate begins:

'I arise today / Through a mighty strength, the invocation of the Trinity,
Through belief in the threeness / Through confession of the oneness
Of the Creator of the Creation.'

Creation and Redemption

One of the most tantalizing references in Patrick's *Confession* is to Christ as *Redemptor*. Was Patrick looking for the redemption of the whole created order as later Celtic spirituality seems to have done? It is impossible to say, though we can be sure that Patrick presented God to his hearers as

'the God of heaven and earth, of sea and river, of sun and moon and stars, of the lofty mountain and the lowly valley, the God above heaven, the God in heaven, the God under heaven.'[17]

The Celts rejoiced in creation and fed upon its glories which were all around them, but they did not exalt it to the neglect of the biblical understanding that it was a fallen creation. They were equally aware of the need for redemption, and the cross held a central place. Again, the high crosses of Ireland are material witnesses to this point. The purpose of God was to restore the whole of creation; grace and nature coming together in a renewed world, 'a world made whole'.[18] This is one of the most popular aspects of the Celtic tradition in the contemporary world, with its emphasis on the environment and Green issues. The Celts are portrayed as a paradigm culture which knew how to think green. They seemed to understand and appreciate the intimate and delicate relationship which humanity has with nature, and indeed they did. But they sought to glorify the Creator through his creation and did not separate them as the modern secular Green movement has done, nor confuse them as the New Age does. Indeed, if we are tempted to quarry the Celtic tradition in support of the environment, we must take into account the whole spectrum of attitudes, including the following:

'Have no care, have no care for the meaningless earth.
Lay no hold, lay no hold on its gaiety and mirth. . . .
The world is running out like the ebbing sea:
Fly far from it and seek safety.' [19]

One of the most frequently quoted legends of St. Patrick is the conversion of the

---

16 A Carmichael *New Moon of the Seasons. Prayers from the Highlands and Islands* (Edinburgh, 1986) p 88.
17 Bamford and Marsh, op cit p 19
18 The title of a book by Esther De Waal, sub-titled *Rediscovering the Celtic Tradition* (London, 1991).
19 Bamford and Marsh, op cit p 83.

daughters of the High King of Tara. When questioned about who the new God was, and where he lived, Patrick replied:

'He has his dwelling round Heaven and Earth and sea and all that in them is. He inspires all, He quickens all, He dominates all, He sustains all. He lights the light of the Sun; He furnishes the light of the light; he has put springs in the dry land and has set stars to minister to the greater lights . . .'[20]

The Celts did not regard the created world as a living, self-regulating being, which many people of New Age persuasion call 'Gaia', the Earth-goddess. They retained a deep reverence for creation, because it is God's creation, and he is present and intimately involved in it. Thus they avoided the rift between Creator and creation which arose in other parts of the West once Christian missionaries had led their converts away from pagan worship of Nature. A strong scriptural doctrine of creation enabled the Celts to appreciate the world in its proper place:

'Learned in music sings the lark / I leave my cell to listen;
His open beak spills music, hark! / Where Heaven's bright cloudlets glisten.
And so I'll sing my morning psalm / That God bright Heaven may give me,
And keep me in eternal calm / And from all sin relieve me.'[21]

Immanence and Transcendence

The Celts were conscious of the nearness of eternity in a way that modern urban and materialist folk have largely lost. Today people visiting Iona are told how the air is 'thin' there, meaning that heaven touches earth in ways which can be discerned with greater clarity than elsewhere. Much Celtic poetry deals with ordinary mundane matters of daily life, but the things of eternity are never far away. The material world invites us to see beyond to deeper spiritual things. The edge of glory is found at the level of the ordinary. This way of seeing arises out of the conviction that it is God's world and he is present in it and can be known. Such a conviction gives eternal significance to everyday things, lighting a fire, milking a cow, rocking an infant to sleep. Even in sleep itself God is close by to protect through the darkness.

'God shield the house, the fire, the kine,
Every one who dwells herein tonight / Shield myself and my beloved group
Preserve us from violence and from harm.'[22]

The immanence of God in his creation is closely related to the incarnational emphasis in Celtic spirituality which appeals strongly to the modern Christian imagination. God is seen as revealing himself in and through his world. One of the most striking emphases in D. Adam's books is the 'presence' of God:

'In the beginning, God. / In the beginning of space. / In the beginning of time. / In the beginning of matter. / In the beginning of our life. / In his creation. / In the heart of each of us.'[23]

20 L Hardinge *The Celtic Church in Britain* (London, 1972) p 104.
21 R Flower *The Irish Tradition* (Oxford, 1947) p 54.
22 Carmichael *New Moon* p 90.
23 D Adam *Tides and Seasons. Modern Prayers in the Celtic tradition* (London, 1989).

The Incarnation means more to the Christian than divine presence in the world. At the heart of the meaning of incarnation is *the* Incarnation, God revealing himself in Jesus Christ. Christ came to be present with us in order to challenge us to change. That the Celts, understanding the reason for the Incarnation is evident in their awareness of human sinfulness and of the need of redemption. St. Patrick, whose experience of Christ was forged through prayer, through the work of mission and through his own suffering, described his Lord in his *Confession* as his companion in suffering, humble and emptied of glory, but one who is also the risen and glorified redeemer.[24]

The sense of God's immanence is thus balanced by a strong sense of divine transcendence. Thus the God who is near is also awesome, the creator of the storm and the winds, the one who was victorious over death and evil at the cross. In a world where the supernatural was never far away, the power of evil as well as good was real.

The Supernatural

St. Bede's stories of the Celtic saints abound with tales of the miraculous. The saints were accorded healing powers; they could control nature: their prayers made the wind change direction to aid sailors or monks, they caused springs to break out; animals and birds served them; they prophesied, saw visions, and battled with Evil.

The battle with Evil was fearfully real for Celtic Christians seeking converts from paganism. They are often praised today because they did not destroy the culture of those to whom they preached the gospel. While this is true, they did not concur with what they found to be incompatible with Christianity. There is much mystique surrounding the druids and their arts, but as well as opposing the Christians, their own religious practices included human sacrifice. The Celtic Christians had to rely on the power of God to combat pagan powers. There are many stories of confrontation between Christians and pagans, battles of naked force. St. Patrick faced the druids at their stronghold at Tara. He and his companions lit the paschal fire on returning to Ireland on the night of the druidical feast of Tara, thus incurring the wrath of the king and his druids. As one of them approached Patrick, reviling the Trinity and the Christian faith, Patrick prayed in a loud voice that God would destroy him. Then he called out verses of Scripture, causing upheaval in the natural world: darkness and an earthquake. The Christians triumphed over their opponents in a story which, however much it is overlaid with legendary embellishment, is clearly presented as a battle between Good and Evil commemorates the event, and illustrates the need to be confident in the power of God:

'At Tara today in this fateful hour / I place all Heaven with its power,
And the Sun with its brightness / And the Snow with its whiteness
And Fire with all the strength it hath / And lightning with its rapid wrath...

---

24 O'Donoghue, op cit p 102.

All these I place /By God's almighty help and grace,
Between myself and the powers of Darkness.'[25]
Christians have often fallen into two camps where the supernatural power of
Evil is concerned; either ignoring it as an outmoded concept, or seeing it on
every corner and behind every problem. Today, Spiritual warfare is on the agenda
of many churches, where the awareness of 'principalities and powers' as spiritual forces is taken seriously. It is seen as relevant where evangelism is concerned, and, given the upsurge in interest in the supernatural outside the Church,
the Celts may have important lessons for us to learn.[26] They recognized the reality of evil, and the conflict which ensued was a conflict in Creation at large and
also in the life of the individual. They found strength in the risen Christ, the
great High King who had triumphed over evil, and who was a power to be
reckoned with.

Prayer
It is the prayers of the Celtic tradition which have caught the modern Chris-
tian imagination and which are assumed to be transmitting the spirituality of
the original Celtic Christians. Prayer certainly pervaded the lives of the early
Celtic Christians. They frequently survive for us as songs and poems written
down from oral tradition, and have a lyrical quality, line balancing line, fre-
quent repetition, sometimes taking the form of a litany.
'God to enfold me, God to surround me,
God in my speaking, God in my thinking.
God in my sleeping, God in my waking,
God in my watching, God in my hoping.
God in my life, God in my lips,
God in my soul, God in my heart.
God in my sufficing, God in my slumber,
God in mine ever-living soul, God in mine eternity.'[27]
Loricae or breastplates were prayers of protection common in ancient Ireland
before Christianity came, and were taken over by the Church. They reflect the
Celtic vision of human life as menaced by evil forces, but the Christian faith
taught that the power of the risen Christ was greater still. The most well-known
is the hymn the 'Breastplate of St. Patrick', mentioned above. Like the follow-
ing, it expresses the conviction that God is both mighty and near to protect:
'The compassing of God and his right hand
Be upon my form and upon my frame;
The compassing of the High King and the grace of the Trinity
Be upon me abiding ever eternally /Be upon me abiding ever eternally.'[28]

25 Bamford and Marsh, op cit p 54.
26 cf A Bowsher *Demolishing Strongholds: Evangelism and Strategic-level Spiritual Warfare* (Grove
    Booklets on Evangelism 21 (Grove Books, Bramcote, 1992).
27 Carmichael, op cit p 15.
28 ibid p 75.

Encircling prayers in the tradition of the *loricae* are among the most popular type of prayers used today, some old, some new:
  'Circle me Lord / Keep protection near / And danger afar
  Circle me Lord / Keep hope within / Keep doubt without
  Circle me Lord / Keep light near / And darkness afar
  Circle me Lord / Keep peace within / Keep evil out.'[29]
The prayers of the Celtic Church are notable for the scope of their subject matter. They cover every aspect of life from cradle to grave, from rising to going to sleep, from milking the cow to laying the fire.
  'I will kindle my fire this morning
  In the presence of the holy angels of heaven...

  'God kindle Thou in my heart within / A flame of love to my neighbour,
  To my foe to my friend, to my kindred all...
  To the brave, to the knave, to the thrall,
  O Son of the loveliest Mary / O Son of the loveliest Mary
  From the lowliest thing that liveth / To the name that is highest of all.'[30]

  'As I save this fire tonight / Even so may God save me.
  On the top of the house let Mary / Let Bride in its middle be,
  Let eight of the mightiest angels / Round the throne of the Trinity
  Protect this house and its people / Till the dawn of the day shall be.'[31]

Many of the prayers mention the saints, especially Mary. Their awareness of the closeness of the other world made them feel in touch with the communion of saints. Evangelical Protestants may find this aspect of Celtic Christianity unpalatable. We need to remember that many of the prayers were collected much later, when 'the age of the saints' itself was long past. They represent reflections on those times, and the fact that these individuals made such an impact on Celtic lands.

Since prayer covered every aspect of life, it naturally had an important place in the work of mission and evangelism. St. Aidan taught his monks to meditate on the Scriptures and learn the Psalms as they walked around the countryside of northern Britain, and we may suppose they also prayed as they walked. We have seen how prayer was an effective weapon against the power of pagan religion, and it was central to the lives of the missionary-monks who not only travelled far and wide to preach the Gospel, but also spent long periods apart for prayer and communion with God.

29 *Carmina Gaedelica*, III, p 77.
30 D Adam *The Edge of Glory* (London, 1985) p 8.
31 D Hyde *Religious Songs of Connaught* (London, Dublin, 1906) II. Republished with introduction by D Daly (Irish University Press, Shannon, Ireland, 1972) II p 47.

6
Discipleship and Mission

Arising out of the Celtic conviction that God is involved with his world, came human response. The call to discipleship, to practise the teaching of Christ and to follow him in this life by taking up the cross is a recurring theme in the lives of the Celtic missionaries. Taking up the cross in a hostile world could be very costly, and it accounts in large measure for the strongly ascetic note in Celtic spirituality.

Extreme asceticism was a characteristic of the Eastern Christian tradition. Ireland in the sixth century has been described as 'the outermost ripple of the great monastic movement of the Greek and Coptic churches of the East.'[32] Celtic monasticism often seems to have more in common with the East than the West with its liking for hermits, isolated retreats and feats of endurance. Indeed, St. Antony of Egypt and St. Paul of Thebes often feature on the carved high crosses as evidence of the eastern influence, while monastic texts commend them as models to imitate. Lonely, isolated places were chosen for the siting of monasteries, islands way out in the Atlantic, such as Skellig Michael, where physical endurance could be tested to its limits. One of the distinctive features of the history of the early Celtic Church is that the story must be told as an account of persons rather than of an institution, for this is how the evidence has come to us. The result is a picture of heroic achievement and dedication to Christ. Indeed the 'Lives' of the saints written by later authors presents the early Celtic saints as direct descendants of the old mythological heroes.

The transforming instrument from paganism to Christianity was the cross. The life of the hermit illustrates the individualism of Celtic Christianity, although it was not expected to be a permanent state. Monks would go off into isolation for a period of time and then rejoin their community. As we have seen, the great missionary monks would do the same. St. Columbanus said:

'You know that I love the salvation of many, and seclusion for myself; the one for the progress of the Lord, that is, of his Church; the other for my own desire.'[33]

St. Cuthbert, who in many ways combined in his person both Celtic and Roman Christianity, had to shoulder many of the judicial duties of bishops within the latter tradition, but still sought the Celtic habit of asceticism and solitude.

Two recurring motifs in Celtic spirituality are pilgrimage and martyrdom, both closely related to the call to take up the cross and follow, whatever the cost. Monasticism was thought of as a form of martyrdom, but there were three different ways of perceiving this role. 'Red' martyrdom was the shedding of blood

---

32 N Chadwick *The Age of the Saints in the Early Celtic Church* (Oxford, 1961) p 60.
33 G S M Walker (ed and trans) *Sancti Columbani Opera* (Dublin, 1957) pp 28-9 (Epistle, 4,4.)

for Christ's sake. This was the desire of St. Patrick who prayed for the privilege of pouring out his blood for Christ's sake, even if it meant he would be deprived of burial and his body would be torn limb from limb. If the monk could not attain this, he sought 'white' martyrdom by renouncing the world. This was the daily living of the ascetic life for Christ's sake. 'Green' martyrdom was peculiarly Irish and stood for the road of penance for sins. The principle of penance for sin was a strong one and became highly developed. In the seventh century, a reforming movement arose known as the *Ceili Dei* (Servants of God) which tried to revitalize this penitential streak of Irish spirituality. The Celtic monks of Lindisfarne in Northumbria, St. Aidan and St. Cuthbert, were also celebrated ascetics, fasting, praying for long periods with outstretched arms, or praying the Psalms in ice-cold water. The practice of having a soul-friend, an *anamchara*, which is a popular feature of much modern Protestant as well as Catholic spirituality, was to aid penance and confession. Whatever the motives love of Christ, the 'folly of the cross', determination to discipline the flesh, or a mixture of all these the Celtic Christians were not content with a superficial faith which did not affect their lifestyle.

Such determination to subdue the flesh has prompted the claim that there was a Pelagian streak at work in Celtic spirituality, an emphasis on the part played by the individual in gaining salvation. Pelagius said that perfection was attainable and it was therefore the Christian's duty to strive to achieve it. Likewise, the Celtic regard for the created order has been seen as contrasting with the deep pessimism of St. Augustine, Pelagius' great opponent. Studies of the theology of St. Patrick, however, have shown how closely it reflects Catholic sources for the Pelagian controversy. The Celts were in general uninterested in theological debate.

They were certainly concerned about orthodoxy, but the repeated emphasis is on doctrine lived out in life and experience. St. Columbanus stated that the Christian life was to be lived, not theorized and debated.

'Green' martyrdom also involved leaving one's native land to become a *peregrinatus*, a perpetual wanderer in the world. Some have seen the motive for becoming a *peregrinatus* as having more to do with a spirit of adventure than with the desire to spread the gospel. But it seems strange to think of these Celtic Christians, who had served Christ at home, not serving him abroad by sharing the gospel. The more likely explanation is that the natural tendency to pursue a life of wandering took on a new purpose through the gospel message. The *peregrinati* set out with no particular destination in mind, but wherever they found themselves they preached Christ and sought to live out the gospel. The 'Lives' of the saints frequently state that pilgrimage was undertaken 'for the love of God, . . for the name of Christ . . . for the salvation of souls and to attain heaven.' Thus there may well have been a strong personal motivation propelling these men out into strange and hostile lands. Certainly the names most well remembered—St. Patrick, St. Aidan, St. Columba and St. Columbanus—were all famous as missionaries who travelled far.

St. Patrick's *Confession* is a lengthy defence of his mission to the Irish. In it he explains that he received divine grace in order that:

' . . . I, though ignorant, may in these last days attempt to approach this work, so pious and wonderful; that I may imitate some of those of whom before the Lord long ago predicted (that they) should preach his gospel "for a testimony to all nations" (Matt. 24.14) before the end of the world.'[34]

We have already seen how St. Patrick modelled himself on the apostle Paul, who devoted his Christian life to the work of mission. Patrick's call to Ireland as described in his *Confession* resembles that of the apostle to Macedonia recorded in Acts 16.9f:

'And then I saw, indeed, in the bosom of the night, a man coming as it were from Ireland, Victorius by name, with innumerable letters, and he gave one of them to me . . . . And while I was reading aloud the beginning of the letter, I myself thought indeed in my mind that I heard the voice of those who were near the wood of Foclut, which is close by the Western Sea. And they cried out thus as if with one voice, "We entreat thee, holy youth, that thou come, and henceforth walk among us."[35]

St. Columba's reasons for leaving Ireland may be shrouded in obscurity, but in doing so he became the archetype of the *peregrinati Christi*. There is moreover, no doubt about the importance of the community he founded on Iona for spreading the gospel in Scotland and the north of England.

St. Aidan, as we have seen, came from Iona to Northumbria in response to a call from King Oswald to evangelise the people there. Bede is full of admiration for him:

' . . . the highest recommendation of his teaching to all was that he and his followers lived as they taught . . . Whether in town or country, he always travelled on foot unless compelled by necessity to ride; and whatever people he met on his walks, whether high or low, he stopped and spoke to them. If they were heathen, he urged them to be baptized; and if they were Christians, he strengthened their faith, and inspired them by word and deed to live a good life and to be generous to others.'[36]

St. Columbanus left Ireland to preach the Gospel abroad in a highly symbolic manner, accompanied by twelve companions. He wrote to his disciples in Luxeuil, after being forced to leave and said:

'It was in my wish to visit the heathen and have the gospel preached to them.'[37]

All this amounts to evidence of a practical spirituality. The Celts took seriously the call to take up the cross and follow Christ. It was a call which involved mission and evangelism, and a life of dedicated holiness.

---

34 O'Donoghue, op cit p 34.
35 ibid p 23.
36 Bede *A History of the English Church and People* (Penguin, London, 1968) ch 5, p 148.
37 G S M Walker, op cit pp 30f.

7

Interpreting Celtic Christianity for Today

In his study of the history of spirituality and the way it may be usefully employed to meet contemporary needs, Philip Sheldrake highlights a number of criteria which must be met if we are not to do violence to a particular tradition. These are:

1. Some knowledge of the historical context, the circumstances in which it arose;
2. In the case of a literary text providing the basis of a tradition, we need some awareness of the basic insights of literary criticism, types of literary genre, understanding of how the meaning of words changes over time and so on;
3. Some understanding of hermeneutics, including a theory of interpretation that will give us an understanding of the unfamiliar in terms of the familiar;
4. We need some idea of how the tradition has developed and been interpreted;
5. We need to recognize the limits of objective historical knowledge: for example, that all historical accounts whether contemporary or later, are always partial and subject to the author's bias.

All this will sound very forbidding to the person whose imagination has been captivated by, for example, poetry from the Celtic tradition, for it suggests that the riches of the Christian tradition must remain inaccessible to all but an elite of scholars. This need not be the case, as we have already seen. This booklet has attempted to explain some of the problems involved in recovering the historical Celtic Church. I have tried to indicate the limits of objectivity where the Celts are concerned and show how the tradition has developed over the centuries.

Any course or workshop using the Celtic tradition, or any other, should seek to mediate the insights of scholarship in a relevant, accurate and intelligible way. Since many people encounter the variety of the Christian tradition through such courses and workshops, this seems a reasonable request, and one which should go a long way towards bridging the gap between our own world and that of the past. There will be others, however, who discover the Celtic tradition through the plethora of books which adorn the shelves of Christian and indeed secular bookshops. It is not unusual to find a 'New Age' or 'spirituality' section in high street bookshops up and down the country. How can people browsing here be helped to discern what the Christian traditions are about? Christians will also be concerned to know which literature is helpful and which is not.

We cannot separate doctrine from spirituality, and indeed those who have been inspired to heights of worship through contemplating the deep truths of Christian doctrine would testify to its role in deepening a personal walk with God. But some understanding of basic Christian teaching is also vital, to enable people to construct a framework of doctrine to guide them through the maze of philosophies vying with each other for attention in the modern world. Without such a framework there can be no yardstick against which alternatives may be measured. Vagueness about what is Christian and what is not will inevitably lead to confusion. In order to enter fruitfully into the unfamiliar, we need a real sense of where we belong.

It is the Church's task to combat the confusion of New Age beliefs with clear teaching and encouragement towards finding a Christian spirituality which is relevant for today. The riches of the Church's inheritance are more than sufficient to bridge the gulf of spiritual emptiness experienced so widely and filled so quickly by other gods.

It is as important to be aware of the contemporary world, its culture, presuppositions and concrete realities, as it is to understand the past, if the two are to engage with any meaning. From the Christian perspective, this involves having a sense of what the gospel is saying to the contemporary situation. Where we can see God at work in other times and places, there is an incentive to find ways of proclaiming the gospel to today's world by drawing from the wells of spirituality in history. It is the same Lord who inspired Aidan and Patrick whom we seek to proclaim.

Christian writers on themes to do with spirituality have an important role. The temptation when compiling any anthology is to select according to a preconceived plan, and this appears to have happened with Celtic material because it lends itself to a number of contemporary themes. What has to be remembered is that there is a great deal left out. Not all anthologies of Celtic prayers and books about Celtic spirituality set out to recreate the world of the Celts in order to offer the twentieth century an 'authentic' experience of another age. Instead they attempt to recapture the spirit of the Celts out of the conviction that the key elements of their spirituality have something to say to the spirit of our own age.

The books of poems, prayers and meditations on Celtic themes by David Adam are composed in the Celtic tradition, using patterns, words and themes which convey the essence of the earlier world of the Celtic Church. In his second book for example, Adam writes a series of meditations based on the hymn of St. Patrick. He freely acknowledges that the hymn itself may belong three centuries after Patrick, but that does not matter. The hymn expresses the early Celtic Christian faith. 'It vibrates still with the God who surrounds us, the Christ who is with us, and the Spirit within us.' This sense of God's presence and power pervading everything may be said to be part of the essence of Celtic Christianity, a principle which shaped the Celtic way of discipleship. It is not of course absent from the consciousness of other parts of the Church throughout history, but it was given a particular expression by the early Celts. Adam is not trying to recover authentic Celtic prayers from the past in his books. Rather he is seeking to reapply the principles of Celtic spirituality to our own day.

8
Engaging with the Celtic Tradition Today

The Celtic saints used the *vox populari* to teach the faith to people. Thus in order to be true to Celtic Christianity we must translate its elements into **modern idiom**. This is what Adam seeks to do. For example, the incarnational aspect must be relevant to the mechanized urban world of the twentieth century. Prayer for us, as for the Celts, must be truly grounded in our daily lives. If the Celts prayed as they squeezed the milk by hand from the cow's udder, we may pray as we press the keys of our computers, ride a bus through the traffic, struggle with bureaucracy, and so on.

Do we reject *culture* as godless and unimportant? The Celts chose transformation. They took what was good and compatible and pointed to Christ through it. For example, the pagan Celts believed passionately in the afterlife as a positive continuance of the whole human personality the Other world was so vividly present all the time, that there were moments when there were no barriers between it and this world at all. As the 'unknown god' in Athens was revealed by Paul's preaching, so the missionaries to the Celts could illuminate the hope of the Resurrection through Christ and the immanence of the living God in his created world.

Go on a Celtic *pilgrimage* and Iona and Lindisfarne are obvious choices, and the journeys across the sea and the causeway add to the sense of a pilgrimage of discovery. Bede's monastery at Jarrow, Cuthbert's tomb at Durham, the abbey of Melrose, Whithorn in Galloway, and of course the crosses and monastic sites of Ireland are all possibilities. Take time to meditate and pray around the themes suggested by the places visited: the nature of the place, the lives of the saints associated with it, and the resolution to return home renewed and more faithful in living the gospel.

We might try writing some *prayers* of our own in the style of Celtic prayers, using the rhythms and balanced phrases which characterize them. Learn to practise the presence of God with David Adam's '5p exercise': Pause, (stop, relax, make space); Presence, (know God is with me the purpose of the exercise); Picture, (what does this Presence mean for me today?); Ponder, (think what it means for each situation just pictured); Promise, (to recall the fact of his presence throughout the day).[38]

The modern **Iona Community** was founded in 1938 by the Revd. Dr. George MacLeod, later Lord MacLeod of Fuinary. It is an ecumenical community of men and women and its purpose, in its own words, is 'to be a sign of the rebuilding of the common life, and to break down the barriers between church and people, between prayer and politics, between the sacred and the secular.' George MacLeod embodied the vision he sought to establish by rebuilding the abbey. It is this Celtic vision of a world made whole, restored, undivided, full of the glory of God which so many contemporary writers on Celtic spirituality are attempting to recapture. Iona's approach to the gospel is radical and uncomfortable, but not unorthodox.[39]

---

38 The exercise is described more fully in D. Adam *The Cry of the Deer* pp 19f.
39 *Coracle*, plus other publications, including songs in the Celtic tradition, may be obtained from: The Iona Community, Pearce Institute, 840, Govan Road, Glasgow, G51 3UU.